P9-DDZ-274

JBIOG
Boyle
Kuslan, Louis

Robert Boyle : the great
experimenter

MORRIS AUTOMATED INFORMATION NETWORK

0 1021 0014996 6

MONTVILLE TWP. PUBLIC LIBRARY
90 Horseneck Road
Montville, N.J. 07045

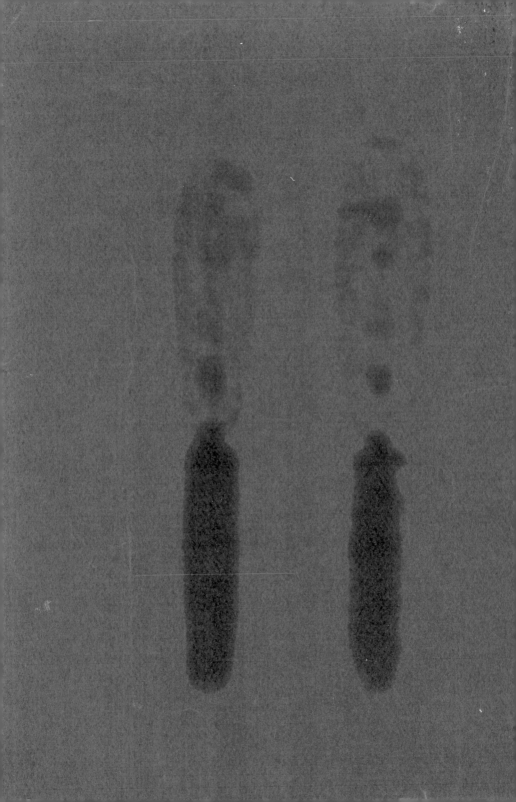

ROBERT BOYLE

The Great Experimenter

By

Louis I. Kuslan and A. Harris Stone

Illustrated by Henry Gorski

History of Science Series
Edited by Derek J. de Solla Price

Prentice-Hall, Inc., Englewood Cliffs, New Jersey

Robert Boyle: The Great Experimenter
by Louis I. Kuslan and A. Harris Stone
History of Science Series, edited by Derek J. de Solla Price

© 1970 by I. Kuslan, A. Harris Stone and Derek J. de Solla Price
© 1970 Illustrations by Prentice-Hall, Inc.

All rights reserved. No part of this book may be
reproduced in any form or by any means, except for
the inclusion of brief quotations in a review, without
permission in writing from the publisher.

Library of Congress Catalog Card Number: 71-122321

Printed in the United States of America. *J*

ISBN-0-13-781468-2

Prentice-Hall International, Inc., London
Prentice-Hall of Australia, Pty. Ltd., Sydney
Prentice-Hall of Canada, Ltd., Toronto
Prentice-Hall of India Private Ltd., New Delhi
Prentice-Hall of Japan, Inc., Tokyo

Introduction

In an age that is dominated by science and technology, it has become necessary that people find out what sort of person it is that becomes a scientist, why and how he does what he does, and what it feels like to make discoveries and inventions. To find out in this way *about* science is a quite different matter from the more ordinary ways of learning the content of science.

If you wish to learn to be a scientist, there are no short-cuts and you must go through all the various theories and techniques that have to be learned. If, however, you want to find out what life would be like if you had successfully been through this learning and emerged as a working scientist, or, if you want to find out what scientists have done and might do as part of the world's work, then a different course must be taken. This different course is to study the history of science. Here one tries to find out why and how scientific discoveries and theories came into being in the ways they did. People have very peculiar and often very wrong ideas about scientists and some of the most important errors can be corrected and some of the most important truths found out by looking carefully at even a small part of the history of science.

In each book of this series, we take just one major scientific incident in the life of a great scientist and find out from this what it felt like to be important at that time and why the advance was great, significant and interesting.

DEREK J. DE SOLLA PRICE

Contents

For Rebecca Kuslan

Chapter One

The Great Experimenter

There were few scientists in Europe in the year 1500, except for teachers of medicine in the universities. By the middle of the 17th century, however, things were much different, for now scientists were employed in many universities. For the first time there was a group of trained professionals who could give all their time and effort to scientific studies. These men were no longer content to accept the time-honored beliefs which had guided man's thought for many centuries. By the year 1600, for example, they had good reason to believe that Aristotle and Ptolemy, Greek thinkers who died many centuries earlier, were wrong in saying that the earth was the center of the universe and that the planets moved in perfect circles around the earth. William Harvey, an English physician, disproved yet another ancient claim which had been proposed by the Greek physician, Galen, in the second century A.D. He showed in 1628 that, contrary to Galen's theory, the blood did not flow from the right side of the heart directly to the left side through holes in the wall which separated the two sides. Instead, Harvey was able to prove that the blood circulated throughout the body from arteries to veins and returned to the heart to be pumped out again.

The new scientists went far beyond overthrowing doctrines which had long been accepted—they invented new sciences such as electricity and magnetism.

Many educated men refused to admit that these new ideas had any value. They were certain that nothing of worth could be added to the knowledge which had come down to them from the ancient philosophers. These men believed that their world could be explained by the laws and principles which were already known. They thought that it was their duty to use what was already known in order to show what God's purpose had been in creating the world. The scientists, on the other hand, were attracted by new ideas. They were irresistibly drawn on by the search for knowledge for its own sake.

They soon realized that experimentation and observation were both useful and necessary tools in this search. Although it is true that people had performed experiments long before the 17th century, they had not relied on their results in deciding whether or not a particular idea was correct. All too often, their experiments were not carefully done, and the "facts" which were gathered were carefully selected by the experimenter to "prove" his point. Even the new scientists often failed to realize the importance of careful experimentation and exact observation in testing hypotheses. We will see that Robert Boyle, the great Irish scientist, was one of the best of these experimenters. His methods and results helped greatly to improve experimental science.

Although experimentation is very old, the growth of science based on experiments was slow. It was not until the number of professional scientists increased in the 17th century that rapid progress in science was made. The changes in man's thinking which resulted from this explosion of knowledge were so dramatic that historians have called the 17th century the "Scientific Revolution." The "Scientific Revolution" was the time when astronomers, physicists, chemists, and biologists first realized that experimentation, aided by such newly invented instruments as the telescope and the barometer, could lead them to the discovery of new phenomena, and could help them propose powerful theories to explain these phenomena.

In addition to discovering new facts which challenged established ideas, scientists began to apply mathematical analysis to their problems. They searched for simple mathematical laws to describe the results of their experiments. This kind of mathematical study, which was characteristic of such men as Galileo Galilei and Johannes Kepler around the beginning of the 17th century, created a new astronomy which completely changed man's understanding of the universe. The triumphs of science were quickly made available to the civilized world by the many books which poured from the printing presses. All who could read could thus become acquainted with the latest results of scientific investigation.

Scholars had also begun to form small groups which met to discuss and to promote learning. One of the first of the scientific societies organized for this purpose was the Accademia dei Lincei (The Academy of the Lynxes). The Academy was founded in 1603 in Rome. The lynx, which is a type of wildcat, was chosen to symbolize a clearer vision—an ability which came from studying science. With a break of a few years, the Academy of the Lynxes held meetings for thirty years under the sponsorship of Duke Federigo Cesi, who was himself a student of natural history. The members met often to criticize and judge the results of their own investigations. Galileo, the best known member of this society, proudly spoke of his membership despite the fact that the group was sometimes suspected of practicing arts which bordered on witchcraft.

One of the most famous of the early societies was the Accademia del Cimento (The Experimental Academy) in Florence, Italy. This Academy lasted for ten years, 1657-1667, under the patronage of the Grand Duke of Tuscany. Its main function was to test the ideas of Galileo and of his students, Torricelli and Viviani, although the nine members had many other interests. The members enjoyed the use of excellent equipment and instruments for their research in what was probably the first physics laboratory in Europe. Their work was published in a book called *Saggi di Naturali Experienze* (Trying Experiments with Nature). This book helped change the styles of experimentation for testing scientific ideas. Through the influence of these societies and the spread of scientific knowledge by means of the printed book, the growth of the new science was rapid. The educated man of 1675 had both a different picture of the world and different ways of gathering and of interpreting information than a man of 1375. These new ways of studying the environment are well illustrated by the work of Robert Boyle, the Irish nobleman, whose experiments are described in this book.

One of the best examples of the way in which the new scientists influenced Robert Boyle's investigations can be seen in a famous experiment proposed by Evangelista Torricelli (1608–1647), an Italian physicist, who studied with the great Galileo and who was a leading member of the Accademia del Cimento. This experiment may have been suggested by an observation which Galileo had once made. He noted that water pumps were unable to lift a column of water more than 34 feet. Galileo was puzzled by this fact. The accepted explanation for the lifting action of a water pump at the time was the statement that "Nature abhors a vacuum." This meant that as the pump acted to form a vacuum, water was pulled or sucked up to fill the space so that a vacuum could not form.

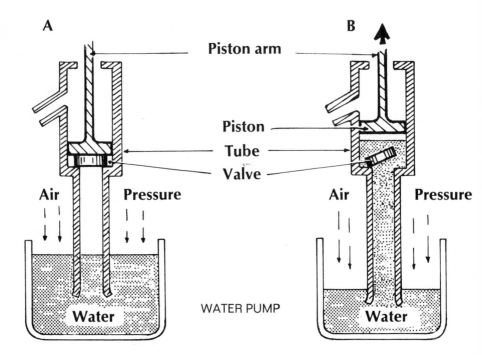

WATER PUMP

"A" is a diagram of a simple water pump before it begins to work. "B" shows the pump in action. When the piston arm is pulled up, the valve opens and the water rushes up the pipe, through the valve, and into the tube. The traditional explanation of how the water rose was that the air in the pump tube was pushed up by the piston arm, and therefore there was no air in the space. Because "Nature abhors a vacuum," the space was immediately filled with water which was sucked up through the pipe. The force of the water pushed open the valve, and the water rushed in to fill the space. As the piston rose higher, the water also rose until it poured out of the pump spout.

Why, Galileo asked, should this "abhorrence of a vacuum" be only strong enough to raise water 34 feet? How could this be explained?

This question was answered by Torricelli, who proposed a much better hypothesis. Torricelli believed that the earth's atmosphere had weight, even though he was unable to prove this idea at first. If it were true that the atmosphere had weight, he thought, it was a reasonable guess that its weight was great enough to *push* the water up. This seemed to him to be a much more sensible explanation of what happened.

In the year 1643, Viviani, who was a close friend of Torricelli, tried an experiment which Torricelli

7

had suggested to test his hypothesis. Viviani took a glass tube which was about a yard long and an inch wide and which was closed at one end. He filled the tube to the brim with mercury, thus forcing out all the air in the tube. Then he covered the open end tightly with a finger and turned the tube upside down. He carefully lowered the tube, finger still tightly pressed over the opening, into an open dish of mercury until the mouth of the tube was well below the surface of the mercury in the dish. Then, he lifted his finger from the mouth of the tube.

THE TORRICELLIAN MERCURY TUBE

Viviani observed that the mercury column which had filled the yard-long tube dropped immediately to a height of 30 inches above the mercury in the dish and remained there. The 6-inch-high space at the top of the tube which seemed to be empty was later called the "Torricellian" vacuum.

Historians of science do not know why Torricelli did not do this experiment himself, or how the idea for it first came to him. He may have heard of a somewhat similar experiment done in Rome three years before. In that experiment, water had been used instead of mercury. Torricelli was probably also aware that Galileo had once suggested that a lift pump should be able to lift mercury as well as water, although the mercury would not rise as high as water. We can only guess that, since mercury is fourteen times heavier than water, Torricelli reasoned that it would rise only one-fourteenth as high, and therefore he would be able to use a much shorter tube in his experiment.

Torricelli had probably guessed even before his great experiment that the earth was covered by a sea of air, and that this air exerted pressure on everything exposed to it. In the year 1644, Torricelli described the experiment in a letter to a friend. In it, he said, "We live submerged at the bottom of an ocean of elementary air, which is known by true experiments to have weight." He was even able to calculate that the atmosphere was at least fifty miles high.

Torricelli insisted that he had created a vacuum in the top of the tube, but few men agreed with him. After all, Aristotle, the famous Greek philosopher, had said that it was logically impossible for a vacuum to exist. He had claimed that "Everything which has volume must be a substance of some kind," and therefore, since a vacuum had volume, it must be a substance and could not be "empty." (This argument was often added to the well-known statement that "Nature abhors a vacuum.")

Torricelli invented a new experiment to strengthen his proposal that the vacuum in the tube was truly "empty." He added water to the dish of mercury from the first experiment and raised the tube with its 30-inch-high column of mercury until its mouth just entered the water which floated on the mercury in the dish. At that moment, the water rushed in and completely replaced the mercury, which poured out into the dish.

Torricelli explained what happened as follows: The vacuum over the mercury in the tube exerted little, if any, pressure on the mercury column. On the other hand, the air pressing down on the surface of the water in the dish exerted enough pressure to push the water into the tube. The water forced in by the pressure of the atmosphere pushed out the mercury. He reasoned that if there had been air in the space above the mercury column, the mercury would

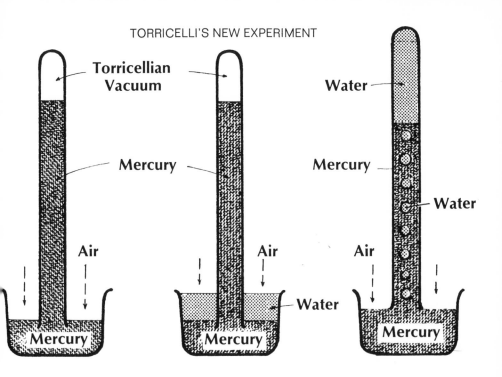

have been forced out by the pressure which the trapped air would have exerted. This idea is easily proven if a little air is pumped into a Torricellian tube. Before the air is added, the pressure of the atmosphere on the mercury in the dish just balances the weight of the mercury in the tube, and the mercury column stands about 30 inches high. As soon as air is forced into the tube, it begins to push down on the pressure of the mercury column. The total pressure of the air and of the mercury column is now greater than the push of the atmosphere on the mercury in the dish, and as a result the mercury column falls.

11

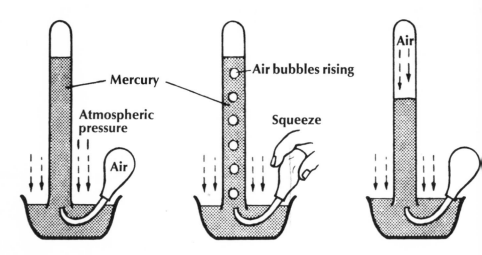

From this and other experiments, Torricelli's argument that he had created a vacuum, a genuinely "empty" space, became much stronger, although the belief that "Nature abhors a vacuum" lingered on for many years.

Early in his research, Torricelli had somehow guessed that the pressure of the atmosphere changed from time to time. He was right, and his glass tube was the first barometer. It became an important instrument for measuring these changes. In clear, dry weather, atmospheric pressure is high, and the mercury column rises. In wet weather the pressure is low, and the mercury falls. Improved versions of Torricelli's barometer are still used today by weather fore-casters. Torricelli did not give the name "barometer" to his instrument. It was Robert Boyle who first called the Torricellian tube a "barometer" about twenty years after Torricelli's experiment.

Soon after Torricelli's discoveries, he wrote to his friend in Rome to tell him what he had done. Within two months, Marin Mersenne (1588–1648) (a Parisian priest and an important disseminator of scientific information at a time when there were no scientific journals) had seen Torricelli's letter and was passing the word along to scientists all over Europe.

When Blaise Pascal (1623–1662), a French mathematician and philosopher, heard of Torricelli's experiments, he was inspired to carry them one step further. He reasoned that if the column of mercury were held up by atmospheric pressure, and if man lived in an "ocean of air," then the closer that one went to the top of that "ocean," the lower the pressure should be. Above sea level, then, the column of mercury which the atmosphere supported should be lower than the 30-inch height of the column at sea level.

To test this hypothesis, Pascal, who was then living in Paris, persuaded his brother-in-law, Florin Perrier, to carry a barometer to the top of the Puy-de-Dôme, a 3,000-foot-high mountain near Perrier's home in Clermont, France. In 1648, despite many difficulties, Perrier completed the experiment. He reported that at the top of the mountain the mercury column stood at about 23 inches, some 7 inches less

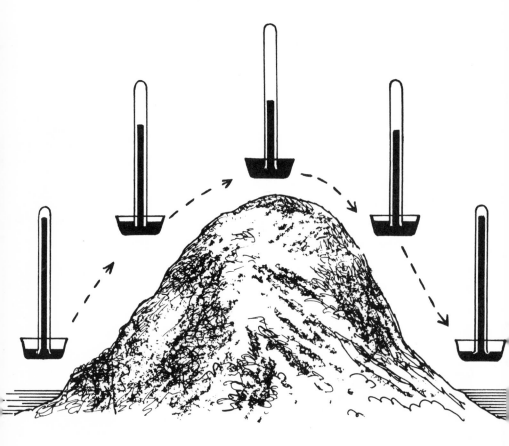

THE MOUNTAIN EXPERIMENT

than at sea level. Halfway up the mountain, the mercury stood at 25 inches. In this way, Pascal and Perrier successfully tested the hypothesis that atmospheric pressure decreases as the altitude increases. This was an additional proof that man lives in an "ocean of air."

Despite the fact that the height of the mercury column was carefully measured on the mountain, the different heights at which these measurements were taken were not accurately known. For this reason, the experimenters were unable to calculate accurately how the height of the mercury column was related to the altitude. Nevertheless, they showed conclusively that the pressure of the atmosphere decreased as the altitude increased.

Within a few years, Robert Boyle (1627–1691), who had been occupied with other kinds of experiments, heard of this experiment on the mountain. He had also learned of a new kind of pump which could take out the air in a container and produce a vacuum. This pump had been invented by Otto von Guericke (1602–1686), the mayor of Magdeburg, who was the first person in Germany to repeat Torricelli's experiments. In 1654, von Guericke produced such a good vacuum in a metal sphere made of two tightly fitting half-spheres that sixteen horses were unable to pull the half-spheres apart.

VON GUERICKE'S EXPERIMENT

Robert Boyle was already one of the leading men in the world of English science. A man of wealth, he was dedicated to the search for new scientific knowledge. He was a skillful and ingenious experimenter, and in his well-equipped laboratory he and his assistants worked tirelessly at many different investigations in chemistry, physics, and biology. His scientific genius, together with this early form of laboratory research institute, allowed him to take full advantage of the new knowledge about the atmosphere which was spreading throughout Europe.

Boyle was so impressed by von Guericke's experiment that he decided to build a better air-removing pump, or, as it was later called, a vacuum pump. He soon realized that with a strong pump, he could create a vacuum in a large container in which experiments could be performed. Von Guericke's pump, however, turned out to be too clumsy for this purpose.

Fortunately for Boyle, one of his assistants was Robert Hooke (1635–1703), who had been a student at Oxford University when Boyle came to this famous university town to establish a laboratory. Hooke's brilliance as an experimenter soon came to Boyle's attention, and Hooke was soon hired to help Boyle. His ingenious experiments were so impressive that in 1662, when the "Royal Society of London for Promoting Natural Knowledge" was chartered by the King, Hooke was made "Curator of Experiments." He was given the duty of inventing and demonstrating "considerable experiments" to the members of the Society at their weekly meetings, a function which he performed admirably throughout his long life.

As "Curator of Experiments," Hooke was probably the first paid experimental scientist, even though his small salary was rarely paid. In addition to the weekly demonstrations to the Society, he carried out research at the request of the members. For much of this time, he served as the Surveyor for the City of London, as a special lecturer on mechanics (for which he was never paid), as a Professor of Geometry, and as curator for the Society's collection of animal, plant, and mineral specimens.

Despite the enormous demands on his time and energy, Robert Hooke made many important contributions to science and technology. His book, *Micrographia*, was one of the most important scientific books of the 17th century. In it, he demonstrated the worth of a new instrument, the microscope, in extending man's senses. He was the first to use the word "cell" to describe the "spaces" in cork which he had seen through his microscope.

Science could not move ahead without suitable tools, and Robert Hooke deserves credit for improving nearly every scientific instrument of his time. Hooke's name is commemorated by Hooke's Law. One form of this law states that if a spiral spring is pulled down by a weight, it will be pulled down twice as far by doubling the weight. Added weight extends the spring proportionately until the spring becomes permanently stretched.

Boyle gave Hooke the job of improving the vacuum pump, and the pump which Hooke put together turned out to be far more than just a better instrument. It was the first "big machine": a sophisticated forerunner of the giant electric-spark generator, the telescope, the "atom smasher," and the electronic computer—"machines" which have become increasingly more important in scientific research.

Hooke's vacuum pump was a model of careful and precise workmanship. It was so good that it set an example which was unsurpassed for many years. The parts, such as the valves, the pumping cylinder, and the leather washer which pushed the air out of the pumping cylinder, had to be tight and strong, fitting precisely so that air could not leak in to spoil the vacuum. There were many other practical problems which had to be solved, or, at least, made less troublesome. For example, Boyle wanted to use a large glass container or receiver so that he could watch the progress of his experiments. Unfortunately, the glass workers in England were unable to make a container larger than seven-and-a-half gallons. The experimenters had to settle for a receiver that was too small and improperly shaped.

The apparatus for each experiment was lowered through a 3-inch-wide hole in the container, and then the container was sealed with a brass plug. Unfortunately, the experimenters were not able to make this seal completely airtight, and air which leaked in around the plug and from other parts of the pump

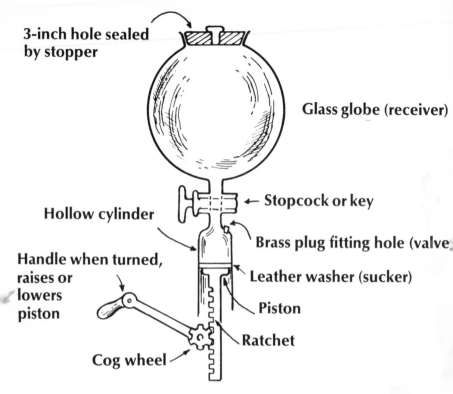

3-inch hole sealed by stopper

Glass globe (receiver)

← Stopcock or key

Hollow cylinder

Brass plug fitting hole (valve

Handle when turned, raises or lowers piston

Leather washer (sucker)

Piston

Ratchet

Cog wheel ⌐

THE AIR PUMP

continued to trouble them. Despite these difficulties, the pump's design and construction were so good that spectacular results were soon obtained.

In one of the first experiments with the new pump, Boyle placed a barometer (Torricellian tube) inside the glass receiver and started the pump. Boyle had reasoned (as did Pascal before him) that if the air pressure pushing down on the mercury in the dish were to be removed, the mercury column of the barometer would fall. In this way he would be able to test the hypothesis that the mercury column of the barometer was held up by air pressure. To Boyle's delight, the mercury column began to fall almost as soon as the pump began to work. It continued falling until it was just barely above the level of the mercury in the dish in which the mouth of the barometer tube was immersed. Boyle believed that the reason the mercury column had not fallen all the way was that some air had leaked in, and this air was enough to maintain a slight pressure on the mercury in the dish.

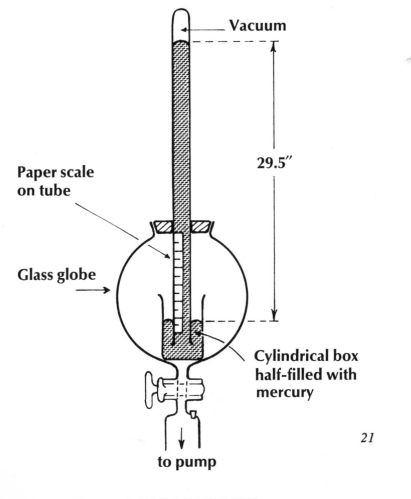

Vacuum

29.5″

Paper scale
on tube

Glass globe

Cylindrical box
half-filled with
mercury

21

to pump

BOYLE'S EXPERIMENT

When Boyle stopped the pump and allowed air to re-enter the container, the mercury column rose. As more air entered, the column soon moved back to its original height of 30 inches. With this ingenious experiment, Boyle was able to "prove" that the mercury column of the barometer was sustained by the pressure of the atmosphere.

He also invented a clever test to see if sound could be carried by a vacuum. Boyle suspended a watch in the glass receiver, with a thin thread holding the watch. As long as air filled the container, the ticking of the watch was clearly heard. As soon as the pump began to remove the air, the sound grew fainter. Before long, the ticking of the watch could no longer be heard. When air was re-admitted, the watch was once again heard. With this experiment, Boyle demonstrated that sound could not pass through a vacuum.

Boyle and his assistants tried many different experiments with the new pump. Most of these experiments were not planned to test scientific hypotheses. In this sense, they were not truly scientific. Occasionally, these experiments failed. Sometimes they gave no new clues to help the experimenters understand the processes of nature.

Despite these failures, Boyle's experiments contributed in a most important way to *pneumatics,* which is the branch of physics concerned with the characteristics of liquids and gases. Many of his original experiments are still demonstrated in science classes to illustrate these principles and facts. Boyle could never have made these discoveries without his experiments. Thinking about air pressure might have led to some new ideas, but thought alone could not substitute for the knowledge which came from careful experimentation and observation.

Once, Boyle took a dry lamb's bladder which was soft and flexible. After squeezing it to force out some of the air which it held, he tied the neck to keep air from entering or escaping, and placed the bladder in the glass container of his pump. The bladder began to swell shortly after the pump began to run. Soon, the bladder was fully expanded, just as if air had been blown into it. Boyle reasoned correctly that the air left in the bladder had expanded as the pressure of the air outside the bladder decreased. When air was re-admitted to the container, the bladder crumpled once again. In other experiments, he produced a vacuum so strong that the bladder swelled up till it burst.

He also demonstrated the great force of atmospheric pressure by first sealing the opening of the container with a flat piece of thin glass. Soon after the pump was started and the pressure inside the

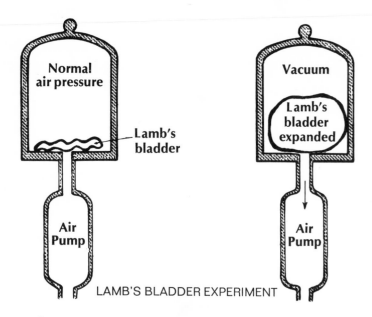

LAMB'S BLADDER EXPERIMENT

container was decreased, the glass plate shattered with a loud noise into thousands of small pieces, which flew into the container. The fact that they were forced *into* the container showed that the force which broke the plate came from the outside air, and not from the vacuum in the container.

Boyle also showed that feathers fell straight down in a vacuum. In the air, they turned and fluttered as they fell. This difference in the way feathers fall, he said, was due to the resistance of the air.

These experiments were fully described by Robert Boyle in a book with the title of *New Experiments Physico-Mechanicall, Touching the Spring of the Air, and Its Effects (Made for the Most Part in a New Pneumatical Engine)*. This book, which appeared in 1660, is one of the most famous scientific books ever published because it gave scientists all over Europe new tools, new techniques, and new ideas for studying natural processes.

Of course, experiments were not new in themselves, although Boyle's use of a sophisticated instrument for his experiments was a new technique. Most "philosophers," as scientists were called in 1660, experimented. However, the books which they wrote about their experiments usually omitted the many details necessary to duplicate these experiments. This was the common practice—either because the writer wished to create a mystery about his work, or because he believed the details were not important.

Boyle's explanations were so detailed, however, that his experiments could easily be duplicated. In fact, they could even be extended to discover new phenomena. Boyle's book was therefore truly revolutionary. Today, all scientists take for granted the idea that enough information must be given to enable other skilled scientists to repeat their experiments. This was not the usual practice three hundred years ago.

As we shall see, Boyle scorned the scientists who wrote and talked so confusingly that no one could understand and profit from their discoveries. His example helped to change the old ways of reporting scientific discoveries and to spread the new science. His book appeared in several languages and circulated throughout Europe. Scientists who did not know of Torricelli's or von Guericke's work or who had thought it unimportant were inspired to follow Boyle's excellent directions. They built their own vacuum pumps, tried his experiments, and invented others.

Despite the great popularity of Boyle's ideas, he soon became the target of strong criticism. Thomas Hobbes (1588–1679), a famous philosopher, and Franciscus Linus, a little-known priest, quickly wrote books attacking Boyle's hypotheses and explanations. Hobbes, however, misunderstood what Boyle had said. He believed firmly that the world was filled with an invisible kind of matter which was even thinner than air. He argued that a vacuum could not be created because this thin matter, which he called the "aether," could not be pumped away. Therefore, the evidence of Boyle's experiments was meaningless. Boyle, he insisted, had *not* made a vacuum!

This is a good example of a kind of thinking which was overthrown by the scientific revolution of the 17th century. People like Hobbes knew, for example, that water did not run out of an inverted bottle with a small opening in the side facing the ground unless the bottle was shaken or a second opening made in it. They explained this fact by claiming that the water could not run out because there was no place for it to go. After all, the space around the bottle was *full* of "aether"! However, as soon as the second hole was made in the bottle, some of the "aether" on the outside passed into the bottle. The water now escaped because there was room for it in the space surrounding the bottle.

To this, Boyle replied that the water could not run out at first because the outside air pushed harder on the opening than did the water in the bottle. The reason for making the second hole was to allow the air to push down on the water in order to force it out of the bottle.

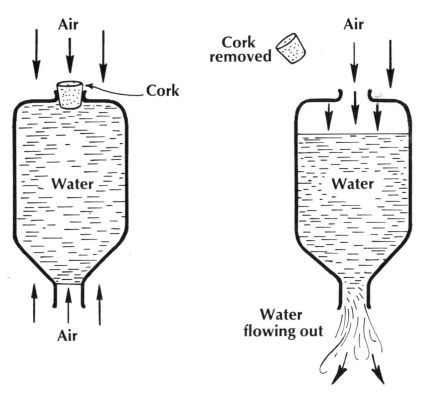

THE INVERTED BOTTLE EXPERIMENT

Boyle's explanation was much simpler than the one Hobbes had proposed. Boyle did not need the hypothesis of an "aether" which, although it filled all space, could not be proven to exist. The "aether" was an assumption based on imagination, not on fact. Boyle chose the simplest explanation based on all the known facts.

Linus' objections to Boyle's theories were even more absurd than Hobbes', yet they were strongly believed by those who refused to accept the reality of the vacuum.

Linus insisted that the mercury in the Torricellian tube was held up by a thin invisible "funiculus" (cord) which was attached to the closed end of the tube and was strong enough to hold the weight of 30 inches of mercury. He said that he could actually "feel" the pull of the "funiculus" when he closed the end of the Torricellian tube with his finger. Linus also claimed, although he had no experimental evidence, that the "funiculus" was just strong enough to pull up 30 inches of mercury. It seems that he was not aware that it *was* possible to raise the mercury column higher than 30 inches.

Boyle answered that the outside air had pushed Linus' finger into the tube and that it was unnecessary to invent an invisible cord which mysteriously sprang into action.

Although this answer seemed to be reasonable, Boyle was not satisfied with it, and he devised several new experiments to show once and for all time that the "funiculus" was nonsense. During this work, Robert Boyle discovered an important law of physics which was soon called Boyle's Law in his honor. This law states that if the pressure on a given volume of gas increases, the volume of that gas decreases in proportion. If the pressure decreases, the gas volume increases in proportion.

Boyle began this series of experiments with a J-shaped glass tube whose short arm was sealed as shown below.

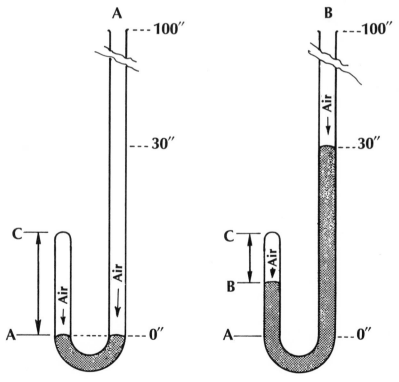

BOYLE'S J-TUBE EXPERIMENT

At the beginning of these experiments, he carefully poured mercury into the tube so that the level of mercury in both arms was equal. *This showed that the air pressure in both arms must be equal to normal air pressure.* The air in the short arm occupied the space between A and C. Then he poured more mercury into the tube until the mercury in the long arm was about 30 inches higher than before. The air in the short arm then occupied the smaller space from B to C. At this point, the pressure of the air in the short arm was equal to twice that of the atmosphere.

This had to be true because Torricelli had already demonstrated that the pressure exerted by a 30-inch column of mercury was equal to normal air pressure. Therefore, when enough mercury was added so that the mercury in the long arm stood 30 inches *higher* than the mercury in the short arm, the *total pressure in the long arm* must have been equal to the pressure exerted by *60* inches of mercury. Thirty inches came from the air pressing down on the apparatus, and 30 inches from the added mercury. Of course, if some of the air trapped in the short arm had escaped during the experiment, the volume of the air in the short arm would have decreased. Boyle and Hooke, however, carefully avoided this possibility. Therefore, the decrease in the volume of air in the short arm must have been due almost entirely to the increased pressure of the added mercury.

Since the air space B-C was only about half of what it had been before, Boyle realized that the volume of the air had been halved when the pressure on that air was doubled. When Boyle poured in more mercury to raise the total height of the mercury column in the long arm to 90 inches, the air space in the short arm was reduced to only one quarter of its original volume. Increasing the pressure on the air by a factor of four decreased the volume of the air to one fourth of its original volume.

Boyle added even more experimental evidence to support his case against the "funiculus." He discovered that if he sucked on the open mouth of the tube, thus decreasing the amount of air pressing down on the mercury, the mercury in the long arm rose noticeably. This happened even if the column of mercury was *90 inches high* and weighed 45 pounds. Linus had pointed out that the "funiculus" could not possibly pull up a mercury column which was longer than 30 inches. Therefore Boyle could safely assume that the funiculus was not responsible for the results of these experiments. In fact, it was only a product of Linus' imagination.

Boyle's explanation of his suction demonstration was as convincing as it was simple. By suction, he had reduced the air pressure on the mercury, and thus decreased the total pressure on the air trapped in the short arm. The trapped or compressed air in the short arm, then acting much like a spring, forced the mercury back down the short arm and up into the long arm. The clear explanation has stood the test of centuries since Boyle's time.

A shortened table of Boyle's original volume and pressure measurements from the J-tube experiment are given below:

Volume of Air in Short Arm	Observed Height of the Mercury Column Above the Beginning Level	Atmospheric Pressure on the Mercury
48 units	00 inches	29 2/16 inches
44 units	2 13/16 inches	29 2/16 inches
36 units	10 2/16 inches	29 2/16 inches
24 units	29 11/16 inches	29 2/16 inches
16 units	58 2/16 inches	29 2/16 inches
12 units	88 7/16 inches	29 2/16 inches

Total Pressure on the Air in the Short Arm (Sum of B & C)	Predicted Height of the Mercury Column Above the Beginning Level in the Long Arm
29 2/16 inches	29 2/16 inches
31 15/16 inches	31 12/16 inches
* 39 5/16 inches (should be 39 4/16 inches)	38 7/8 inches
58 13/16 inches	58 2/8 inches
* 87 14/16 inches (should be 87 4/16 inches)	87 3/8 inches
117 9/16 inches	116 4/8 inches

*These were Boyle's errors in addition.

When the volume of air in the short arm was 48 units, and the level of the mercury in the two arms was equal, the pressure of the atmosphere on the mercury in the long arm must also have been equal to the pressure of the mercury on the air trapped in the short arm. If they had not been equal, the level of the mercury in the two arms would have been different. These pressures, he reasoned, must have been equal to the pressure of the atmosphere, which he observed to be 29 2/16 inches of mercury.

The figure below shows how these numbers were obtained.

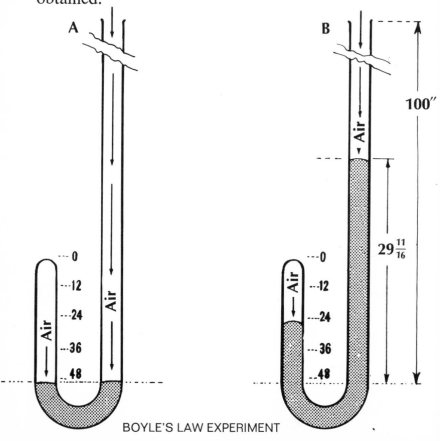

BOYLE'S LAW EXPERIMENT

Then he poured enough mercury into the long arm to force the mercury column in the short arm up 24 units, leaving 24 units of air trapped in that arm. He found that the additional mercury needed was 29 11/16 inches. The total pressure on the 24 units of air in the short arm was 58 13/16 inches, of which 29 2/16 inches was due to the pressure of the atmosphere, and 29 11/16 inches came from the added mercury. Fifty-eight and 13/16 inches is about twice the original pressure of 29 2/16 inches, and the volume of 24 units is just half the original volume of 48 units. Therefore, when the pressure was doubled, the air in the short arm took up only one half of its original volume.

Guessing that this relationship was constant, Boyle calculated what the pressure should be for each new volume. Table 1 shows that his predictions were not far different from his experimental results. Even at the greatest pressure he could reach—and despite the errors caused by leaks, escape of water from the mercury into the air space, readings to an accuracy of only an eighth of an inch, a few errors in addition, and temperature changes which affected both the volume of the air and the height of the mercury column—the difference between the predicted and the experimental figures was only about one percent. This agreement between what was predicted and what was observed impressed all who studied his work.

One way of writing Boyle's Law is $PV = k$. This simply means that (P) the pressure on a gas such as air, when multiplied by (V) the volume of that gas, is equal to (k) a constant amount. If the *pressure increases*, the *volume decreases* by just enough so that the product of the pressure and volume is unchanged. If the *pressure* is *decreased*, the *volume increases* proportionately, so that the product remains the same.

If we test the data by actually multiplying the numbers in Table 1 to see if P times V is constant, it is obvious that this is not the case. For example, the original volume of 48 units times the pressure of 29 2/16 inches of mercury is 1,398. The final volume of 12 units times 117 9/16 inches of mercury pressure is 1,411.

Boyle's work was certainly not completely accurate, and therefore his results did not fully justify the law. Nevertheless, there is no doubt that Boyle's experiments led to the discovery of a true law of nature. Perhaps more important than the law, however, is the fact that for the first time, scientists were presented with an honest and reasonably accurate set of experimental results. It was a shock for them to have to accept the idea that a natural phenomenon could be represented by this approximately true table of numbers. In the past, experimental results had usually been adjusted by the experimenter so that his results "proved" an already accepted hypothesis. Boyle's work shows no evidence of this kind of "proof." However, his example failed to change the accepted ways of presenting experimental data. Not for many years to come was experimental work of equal quality required of scientists.

Boyle never said that his law could be applied universally and under all conditions. He was much too cautious a scientist to make such a claim. He was content that within the limits of his apparatus and methods, the law fit the facts to a reasonable extent.

In one sense, Robert Boyle was not the real discoverer of the law named in his honor. He was not the first to do this particular experiment, but he was the first to suggest it and to describe how it should be done, and it is because of this that it is called Boyle's Law. The use of a man's name in an eponym, as it is called, is a sign that the scientific community has recognized his intellectual property. Several other men, including Robert Hooke, performed similar experiments, acting on Boyle's suggestions. A few years later, Edme Mariotte (1620–1684), a Frenchman, independently discovered this gas law. In France, Boyle's Law is still called Mariotte's Law in his honor. The independent discovery of scientific laws and principles, of which this is a good example, has happened many times in the history of science. One of the most famous examples is the almost simultaneous invention in 1886 of an inexpensive process for producing metallic aluminum by Charles Hall in the United States and Paul Heroult in France. Both men were 21 years of age at the time, and both developed nearly identical methods of separating aluminum from aluminum oxide by passing a strong electric current through it.

Scientists now know that Boyle's Law is not by any means exact, although it works quite well for most gases at normal temperatures and pressures. Countless numbers of students have learned Boyle's Law and its many applications to chemistry, physics, and biology. Important as these applications are, they are insignificant when compared to the great influence of Boyle's efforts to show how the workings of nature can be explained without depending on mysterious and untestable powers. He convinced men of his time that they could give reasonable and simple mechanical explanations of the world around them. In particular, by understanding the physical properties of air and the vacuum and by his experiments on them he left the way open for the discovery of gases and vapors. These were concepts that helped transform alchemy into the science of chemistry. This new way of thinking was influential in forming the scientific mood of the years to come, and it provided a bold example of how man's striving for knowledge could be channeled into new and sensible forms.

Chapter Two

The Chemist

Robert Boyle was irresistibly drawn to the wonders which he saw all around him. He examined closely the structure and the actions of living things, such as the blood vessels and the flow of blood, and the movement of liquids in plants. But he was just as interested in studying the winds, the oceans, the stars and planets—indeed, every bit of the world known to 17th-century philosophers.

His one real love, that to which he always returned after straying to the other sciences, was chemistry, a science which had fascinated many men before him and was to attract many more afterward. Boyle often told his friends that he had been "bewitched" by chemistry. His laboratory was an enchanted island where he spent every moment he could spare.

THE ALCHEMISTS

Chemistry could hardly be called a science during the 17th century. Few learned men gave it a moment's thought, for they were certain that chemistry could never help them to better understand the world about them. The alchemists, of course, had been interested in chemistry for many centuries, but for very special reasons. The natural philosophers who were displeased by the claims and mysterious talk of many alchemists, tended to ignore the serious chemists. The philosophers objected because they thought that chemistry lacked a unifying framework of theory which led to new discoveries and to new knowledge. There was, for example, no accurate way of predicting what would happen if different chemicals were mixed. Indeed, there was no reliable way even to identify chemicals. Because of this, the philosopher who could accurately predict the position of the planets from Johannes Kepler's laws believed that chemistry was unworthy of the name of science. Of course, some branches of chemistry were useful, as, for example, for preparing medicines, extracting metals from ores, and making better dyes. These applications were of importance only to medical men or to artisans, and therefore were of little interest to the philosophers.

The men who were known as alchemists were highly skilled in practical chemistry. They had mastered the art of heating solids and liquids in order

to create new substances. They knew how to work with strong acids and alkalis to produce strange materials. Despite the ridicule by philosophers, and fear of their "magic" by the common people, they pursued their chemical studies. Nicholas Lemery (1645–1715), who was an excellent chemist, once said that alchemy was "an Art without any Art, whose beginning is lying, whose middle is nothing but struggle, and whose end is starvation."

The alchemists were as undaunted by such strong comments as they were by years of frustration in searching for the "Philosopher's Stone," by their occasional illnesses brought on by the choking fumes of their poorly ventilated rooms, and the severe burns from the fires which heated their chemicals. The "Philosopher's Stone" was a magical powder whose touch or mere presence was believed to be capable of changing base metals such as lead, mercury, or copper into gold or silver.

Men spent entire lives in search of the wonderful "Philosopher's Stone": There are many stories about their overpowering belief in its existence. For example, a Belgian chemist named Jan Baptista van Helmont (1579–1644) was well known by Robert Boyle, who thought he was sensible and competent. Van Helmont, however, explained in a long and confusing book how he had changed a large amount of mercury into gold with a tiny bit of the "Philosopher's Stone" which a stranger had given him. Although many alchemists were cheats and tricksters, it is probable that van Helmont fooled himself because he was so obsessed by his desire to make gold. The alchemists wrote many books about their ideas and their chemical practices in their laboratories. These were so mysteriously worded, so confusing and difficult to understand that scientists paid no attention to them. The alchemists clearly did not understand why certain things happened when they heated, boiled, dissolved, distilled, and mixed their chemicals. They lacked an effective theory to explain what these operations did, and they did not understand the nature of the substances with which they worked. Their materials were usually so impure that the alchemists often failed to get the same results when their experiments were repeated. Then too, the alchemists tried to keep each other from learning their "secrets." Their books, therefore, were purposely vague, and were written more to gain personal fame than to inform. The man who wished to learn chemistry could gain little from studying the work of alchemists. The alchemists, however, without really trying, made a number of valuable chemical contributions by discovering such new chemicals as hydrochloric, nitric, and sulphuric acids, and alcohol. They also discovered many salts such as silver chloride and potassium arsenate.

THE IATROCHEMISTS

Besides the alchemists, a second group of chemists flourished during the 16th and 17th centuries. These were the iatrochemists or medical chemists whose goal was to prepare new medicines through chemistry. Theophrastus Bombastus von Hohenheim, usually called Paracelsus (1493–1541), was the founder of this group. Although Paracelsus believed in the "Philosopher's Stone," he devoted his life to reforming the traditional methods for curing illness.

Paracelsus and his followers prepared many compounds of antimony, mercury, lead, and copper, which they gave their patients. These medicines sometimes helped. The patients occasionally recovered, perhaps in spite of, rather than because of the treatment. Their poisonous drugs must have shortened many lives. Nevertheless, many new chemical facts were learned because medicines were prepared in many different ways. This knowledge was put to good use by future generations of chemists.

Robert Boyle was greatly influenced by the ideas and discoveries of the iatrochemists. Not only did he profit from their skill in preparing chemicals, but he firmly believed in the medicinal values of their preparations. Throughout his life, he dosed himself with medicines that he or his friends had prepared.

INDICATORS

One of Robert Boyle's most important investigations was the fascinating and immensely useful experiments with chemical "indicators." Indicators are substances which change color in the presence of acids or alkalis. Almost every boy or girl who has a home chemistry laboratory has used indicators such as litmus paper and phenolphthalein. If a drop of acetic acid (the acid in vinegar) is placed on blue litmus paper, the litmus turns red. If a drop of a washing soda or ammonia solution is placed on the red spot, the blue color returns. A solution of phenolphthalein is colorless, yet a trace of ammonia or sodium carbonate (both alkalis) turns the solution pink. Adding a drop of vinegar (acid) restores the original color.

Robert Boyle was the first chemist to realize that indicators were reversible. He discovered that they could change from acid to alkaline forms under the right conditions, and that the color of the acid form was quite different from that of the alkaline form. There were no tests for whole classes of chemicals such as acids and alkalis, although a few tests for specific chemical substances had been known for hundreds of years. The Roman writer Pliny was said to have known how to test for iron in water by adding a solution of nutgall, which comes from certain plants and which contains tannin. A black color was proof of the presence of iron.

Boyle tested a liquid known as "syrup of violets," which was made by boiling violet petals and then adding sugar to the product. He discovered that acids always turned the blue syrup red, and alkalis turned it green. These colors were reversible upon adding alkali or acid. This test was soon used throughout Europe. Boyle experimented with many other indicators, such as the coloring from other kinds of blue flowers and the juice from purple cabbage.

Most chemists seemed to be unconcerned with the impurities in their chemicals. Although changes in purity caused great differences in results, chemists did not take the time to test for impurities. In the late 16th century, chemists knew that when copper was dissolved in aqua fortis (nitric acid) the solution turned blue. No one knew for certain whether or not silver dissolved in aqua fortis also turned the solution blue, or whether the change in color was due to the presence of copper as an impurity in the silver.

Boyle was well aware of the chemist's need for pure materials. He continually searched for tests to identify his chemicals that were more reliable than the common tests of color, form, and taste. He was particularly anxious to find a foolproof test for acids and alkalis. Many chemists of his day knew that such acids as "oil of vitriol," "aqua regia," "spirit of vine-gar," and "aqua fortis" bubbled vigorously when potash (potassium carbonate) was added to them. Boyle, however, was the first to discover that acids always tasted sour. If a substance thought to be an acid failed to bubble when it was poured on some potash, and if it were not sour to the taste, it could *not* be an acid.

One of his best demonstrations was with alkaline liquids such as ammonia, and with alkaline solids such as potash. Each, in solution, was colorless. When a chemical named mercury sublimate (mercuric chloride, a deadly poison) was added to the alkaline liquids, their solutions turned white. The alkaline solid, in comparison, turned orange. This was an important discovery, for it gave chemists a new and more reliable way to identify the different kinds of alkalis.

Boyle relied on these and on many other tests to identify and to study the chemicals he synthesized. He always kept these indicators and test materials on hand in his laboratory. He often tested mineral waters for their medicinal value, looking closely at each sample, sniffing it, tasting it, and checking its density. He distilled it to learn how much solid mat-ter was left behind. He added a gall solution to find iron, and used "syrup of violets" and other indicators to test the acidity of the water sample. With mercury sublimate, he could detect potash if it were present.

After separating the solid matter by distillation, he examined the crystals through a microscope for color and shape. He heated them to see if they melted easily. If the flame turned green, he knew that copper was present.

One of the problems which made chemistry so difficult at the time was the existence of many different names for the same substance. Robert Boyle tried, with some success, to identify a substance on the basis of its general properties and to name it accordingly. Of course, he made many mistakes, especially in the case of the compounds known as salts, which are formed by the action of an acid on an alkali or on a metal. There was no simple way to identify the salts as there was for the acids and alkalis. Boyle knew that copper and iron sulphates were not identical, but he mistakenly believed that the salt that was formed when hydrochloric or nitric acid acted on metals was also a sulphate, not a chloride or a nitrate.

There was no way at that time to solve this problem. There was no theory to which chemists could turn for predictions and explanations. More than a hundred years were to pass before the science of chemistry was to be set on the modern track by Antoine Lavoisier, the great French chemist. However,

Lavoisier's genius would not have been sufficient without Boyle's pioneering efforts in identifying chemical substances.

THE "ICY NOCTILUCA"

One of the finest examples of Boyle's experimental technique and of his great ability to handle primitive apparatus, despite great peril to life and health, occurred when he prepared white phosphorus. He gave it the imaginative name of the "Icy Noctiluca." "Noctiluca" refers to the way in which white phosphorus continuously gives off light. Phosphorus was discovered in 1675 by a German alchemist, Hennig Brand, who was probably the first person recorded by history as having discovered a chemical element. Gold, silver, iron, tin, and lead had been known from prehistoric times and arsenic and antimony had been identified before the beginning of the 17th century, but their discoverers are unknown.

Another German, Daniel Kraft, paid Brand to reveal his secret method of preparing phosphorus. Kraft toured Europe exhibiting this curious glowing substance. Robert Boyle first saw it on display in the court of Charles II in England about 1679, where Kraft displayed both a solid and a liquid which glowed continuously. Kraft refused to tell Boyle how

he had prepared phosphorus, although he did confide to him the fact that it could be made from a substance belonging to the body of man.

Challenged by this information, Boyle and his assistants set to work, and after many weeks they successfully extracted quantities of white phosphorus from human urine. The experimenters were exposed to many dangers, not least of which was the readiness with which white phosphorus burst into flame when exposed to air. Because of its flammability, white phosphorus is stored and handled under water. White phosphorus is also very poisonous. As little as three-hundredths of an ounce taken internally can cause death. In smaller quantities, it causes a disease known as Phossy Jaw, the decay of the jaw bone.

Despite these hazards, Boyle's study of phosphorus was so thorough that for almost 200 years, few observations of importance were added to those he made. He described its form, color, density, softness, and reaction to air. He tasted the water in which it was stored, a dangerous but common test at that time. He studied the solids which were left behind when the water was evaporated. He learned that phosphorus was not particularly soluble in water or acids, but it did dissolve in oil of cinnamon and oil of cloves, both of which then glowed in the dark. When the "Icy Noctiluca" was dropped into alcohol, nothing seemed to happen, but when the alcohol was then poured into hot water, flashes of light appeared.

Boyle investigated the length of time a piece of phosphorus would glow in air. A lump weighing three grains (0.006 ounces) glowed for six days, continually giving off white smoke and a strong odor. He noticed that when phosphorus was burned in a candle flame, it caught fire before the paper on which it was held burned. He discovered that it caught fire if the sun's rays were focused on it with a magnifying glass, and it changed from a white solid into a mixture of white, yellow, and red powders. This product, made up of phosphoric oxides and red phosphorus (a different form of phosphorus), quickly absorbed water from the air and formed a strong acid called phosphoric acid.

Robert Boyle even predicted some uses for his "Noctiluca," although he modestly said:

> The uses, that may be made of noctilucas . . . are not, in all probability, all of them to be easily foreseen and declared, especially by men, who have not yet had time and ability to make those improvements of self-shining substances, that, by the assistance of the father of lights. I hope will, in the process of time, be attained.

To decrease the ever-present danger of explosion in the power rooms of warships, he proposed that his glowing phosphorus illuminate those rooms.

Divers could take it with them to light their way, and to attract fish for fishermen. Those who awakened in the dark could see the hour markings on their clocks. Of course, Boyle was unable to predict the many modern uses of phosphorus—in matches, fertilizers, explosives, metallic alloys, and in manufacturing thousands of important chemicals.

Robert Boyle was a great, ingenious, and inexhaustible experimenter. He believed in the existence of simple materials of which all matter was made, and he explained what he saw in terms of these substances. His explanations were clear, simply expressed without mystical and magical forces. All who could read English could read and understand exactly what he had achieved in his laboratory.

Chapter Three

The Philosopher's Stone

Robert Boyle was certain that chemists could do much more than create new drugs. He was not completely convinced that they would ever find the "Philosopher's Stone," although many chemists accepted the possiblity that they could change base metals into gold. Boyle was ahead of his time in many ways, but he lived in a period in which most educated men believed in alchemy. As we shall see in Chapter IV, Boyle's theory of how substances were formed and changed led naturally to the idea that one element could be converted into another. It was as natural in the 17th century to accept the transmutation or change of metals as it is in the 20th century to accept space travel.

Boyle even exerted his considerable scientific prestige to repeal a law passed more than two hundred years earlier, banning experiments on "multiplying" gold. The new law which he helped write permitted experiments designed to produce gold. However, all gold and silver prepared in this special way would have to be sold to the English Mint. Did Boyle force the repeal of the old law because he thought that the great mystery of transmuting metals would soon be solved by dishonest men? Or, was it because of his strong belief that philosophers should be completely free to unlock the secrets of nature for the benefit of all?

We know that in the year 1676, he claimed in an article published in the *Philosophical Transactions of the Royal Society* that 25 years earlier he had made a special kind of mercury from antimony. After mixing this "mercury" with finely divided gold on his hand, the mixture had become very hot. According to some alchemists, the production of heat was a sign that gold was being formed out of the "mercury." He asserted that this mixture easily passed through leather, even though it was much denser than ordinary mercury. It could be distilled, and after long heating, the "mercury" gave glass a ruby color. Despite the fact that the "mercury" was not yet completely changed into gold, it seemed to Boyle that a major step had been taken. Few details of this process were published because Boyle was worried about the possible effect of his article. He thought that unscrupulous men would try to use his process for their own gain.

The great scientist, Isaac Newton (1642–1727), who also believed in alchemy and was himself an excellent chemical experimenter, wrote to the Secretary of the Royal Society asking that these details never be made public because evil might result. Newton doubted, however, that Boyle had made any progress in transmuting "mercury" to gold. He believed that the heat which appeared when the "mercury-antimony" was mixed with gold could be explained as a simple physical action, like the heat given off when quicklime is added to water.

Robert Boyle was probably deeply offended by this explanation. At any rate, he never published additional details. Soon after, however, he wrote a book only seventeen pages long, whose subtitle is, "A Strange Chemical Narrative." This book, *Of a Degradation of Gold*, is a story of alchemy in reverse, whereby gold is changed into a less valuable metal. Boyle believed that if gold were to be transmuted into a less valuable metal, the reverse could also happen. The main character of this story is "Pyrophilus" (lover of fire), who has been given a strange red powder by a learned visitor to England. Pyrophilus invites a "Doctor of Physic," a man well versed in metalworking, to witness his attempt to change gold by means of the red powder.

The pure gold is melted in a special container, the powder added, and the mixture is heated to a very high temperature and then allowed to cool. The solid in the container no longer resembles gold. It is in the form of a dirty, metallic, rough-edged lump which projects a little button of silverlike metal. This solid no longer gives the usual tests for gold. The touchstone, a black rock which gives a golden streak when rubbed by gold, produces a streak more like that of silver. The mass is no longer soft and malleable like gold. Chemically, its reactions are like those of silver, and its density is less than that of gold.

According to Boyle's book, every test known to 17th-century chemists proved that the gold had been transmuted into a silverlike mass. Although written in story form, the evidence shows that this book was merely a device to avoid embarrassing questions from skeptics like Isaac Newton. Robert Boyle seems to have believed wholeheartedly in the story that Pyrophilus tells: that a small amount of the red powder converted more than a thousand times its own weight in gold into silver.

Why did Boyle accept this transmutation as a genuine experiment? No one knows for certain, but there is an interesting theory that, unknown to Boyle, one of his trusted assistants made certain that the experiment would be successful by secretly replacing the gold with silver. This may have been because the failure of this experiment, which was intended to show that Newton had been wrong in his criticism, would have hurt Boyle deeply. Boyle's many assistants were responsible for nearly all the chemical work of his laboratory. They had many opportunities to falsify the experiments without his knowledge. They were well acquainted with alchemy. They looked up to their master, and probably more than one of them would have "helped" him in this way.

Robert Boyle was much too proud a man and too good a scientist to have deliberately falsified his work. He needed no money, for he was already wealthy. He never sought fame, although he was one of Europe's leading scientists. However, he did believe in transmutation, and he seems to have completely accepted the results as proof of the "mercury" heating experiment performed so many years before.

Boyle was a creature of his times in at least one other way. He was a devoted follower of the iatrochemists, who sought to prepare drugs by chemical means. He suffered from bad health, perhaps aggravated by his habit of dosing himself with these drugs. Because his youthful experiences with medical men were very unhappy, he spent much time inventing new medicines and collecting "recipes" for other drugs from every likely source. He gave a rating of "A" to those "recipes" which were excellent; "B" to those which often helped; and "C" to those which were undependable and to be used only when nothing else helped. The men and women of the 17th century must have been exceedingly rugged to survive this kind of treatment. The medicines ranged from the very poisonous to the completely useless. Boyle, for example, prescribed compounds of mercury and antimony for many diseases. To cure his malaria, he self-prescribed:

> A handful of groundsel (a local plant), shread and cut it small, put it into a square paper bag of about four inches every way, pricking that side that is to be next to the skin, full of large holes. . . . Let the patient wear this upon the pit of his stomach, renewing it two hours before every fit.

The groundsel at least was not intended for internal use. It could not help, but it would not hurt. To cure jaundice, Boyle suggested that the patient hang a sheep's gall bladder, containing a few drops of the patient's urine, over his bed. As the gall bladder dried up, Boyle claimed that the jaundice would disappear "in sympathy." He asserted that some moss which he had been given in Ireland would stop nosebleed if the moss were held in the hand. He always kept a ring made from an elk's hoof by his bedside as a "cure" for the stomach cramps which often disturbed his sleep.

A number of Boyle's colleagues did not accept alchemy and the supposed value of its medicines and charms as uncritically as he did. For some reason, Boyle never applied the same critical analysis to his beliefs in alchemy and in medicine that he applied to the study of air pressure and to chemical indicators. In many matters he was a man of his age, yet he is not to be condemned because of certain uncritical habits. Three hundred years from now, men may look back to our times to laugh at our beliefs that atoms are made up of electrons, protons, and neutrons, and that cancer is best treated by surgery. None of us can escape completely from the beliefs and practices of our society.

Chapter Four

Chemical Theories

Robert Boyle was one of a handful of scientists in the 17th century who thought that chemistry could be very helpful to the natural philosophers. He was dismayed by the reluctance of these philosophers to listen. The philosophers, in turn, thought chemistry was a waste of time, and they were unhappy to see Boyle fritter away his time in an "Art they judge so much below a philosopher, and so unserviceable to him."

Boyle, however, was trying to raise chemistry from its lowly position by changing it into a rational, theoretical, clearly "philosophical" science. He has the honor of being the first to attempt to make a true science of chemistry. He had studied the books of such great scientists and thinkers as Galileo Galilei,

Francis Bacon, Johannes Kepler, and Rene Descartes. Although he was not a highly trained mathematician and avoided the language of mathematics, he was able to understand and to accept their ideas, which were often stated in mathematical terms. The kind of science which they promoted seemed to most philosophers to be completely unrelated to the smoke and flame of the chemist's laboratory. Boyle, however, worked hard to pull chemistry out of the shadows of mystery and magic, and in sight of all, tried to show that even though chemistry was not yet a mathematical science, it would still be of great value to the philosophers.

In the year 1661, Boyle published some essays written between the years 1657 and 1659 in a book called *Physiological Essays*. His purpose was to prove that chemistry offered the most direct way to understand nature's structure. Had not Francis Bacon, whose books he had read and reread once said, "Those who desire to command Nature must understand her"? Why not, he thought, take for this purpose the shortest and most promising road, that of chemistry?

But to *say* that matter must be studied chemically was much easier than to try it. Physics and astronomy were so far advanced that men could predict the positions of the planets from certain laws and principles.

The goal of physics was to understand why certain things happened, and to make testable predictions of future events. Philosophers had already gone far in this direction. Boyle argued that the chemist would soon be able to understand the laws of chemical reactions from his experiments. Knowing these laws, the chemist would then be able to make reasonable predictions. The time would come, Boyle thought, when chemists could predict (if they did not already know) that substances such as potash (potassium carbonate) would turn syrup of violets green, and could explain why vinegar, spirit of salt (hydrochloric acid), and lemon juice were acids.

He argued that chemists could break substances down into elements, and therefore would be able to work with materials which were much simpler than those found in nature. Since the chemist used glass containers, he could see exactly what happened to the materials which he added to the reaction, and he could leave out other materials to see what the result would be. Since chemicals were "active," remarkable changes took place quickly. For these reasons, he urged philosophers to look to chemistry for the help he was sure they would find.

To achieve this goal, it was necessary for theory and experimentation to be blended. Experiments lead to theory. In turn, theory points to new experiments which test the predictions, and eventually the theory itself. These two faces of science are inseparable. Unfortunately, Robert Boyle died more than a hundred years before a suitable theory of chemistry was invented by Antoine Lavoisier. Lavoisier, however, was successful because Boyle's argument that chemistry was a true physical science had long been accepted in France. French chemistry had shifted from medicine and mineralogy to pure chemical problems, such as the reasons for the existence of different chemical substances, their identification, and the prediction of the products of their chemical reactions.

Boyle's ideas were also accepted by the members of the Royal Society of London, one of the most important groups of scientists in Europe. The English chemists, however, specialized in "pneumatic" chemistry, isolating and identifying such gases as hydrogen, carbon dioxide, and oxygen in accord with Boyle's pioneering experiments.

Boyle believed in the existence of atoms, and he became a leader in the movement to explain all chemical and physical actions by the movement of atoms. The idea that all matter is composed of atoms is very old. The Greek philosopher Leucippus (about 450 B.C.) is reported to have believed in their existence. Democritus of Abdera (460–370 B.C.) said that these atoms were tiny and hard, having form and weight, but lacking color, taste, and odor. They continually moved in a vacuum, and when they collided with one another they joined together, held by a sort of "hook and eye" instead of by magnetic or electrical forces.

Another school of thought, believed to have sprung from the great Greek philosopher, Aristotle, was even more widespread. As this philosophy was understood in the 17th century, the vacuum was non-existent. All earthly space was filled with materials of different kinds, all made up of four "elements," *earth, water, fire,* and *air.* Each element had its own special appearance and behavior. The differences between chemical substances were caused by different proportions of these "elements."

A third school of thought, which began with Paracelsus, believed in three quite different elements —*salt, sulphur,* and *mercury.* These names do not refer to salt, sulphur, and mercury as the chemist knows them today, but to some mysterious ghostlike substances which were thought to be the basis of all matter. These three elements, combined in various ways, were held to be responsible for the properties of all substances. For proof, the Paracelsans would point out what happened when a green twig was burned. The liquid which bubbled out was identified as *mercury,* "that acid, permeable, penetrable, ethereal, and pure liquor." The oily matter which flowed out of the twig "proved" the presence of *sulphur,* and the ashes which remained were obviously the *salt.*

The elements in which Aristotle and Paracelsus believed are different in almost every way from the hundred or more elements known today, for they were either imaginary or made up of complicated mixtures of true elements. The 17th-century chemists believed that these elements were real, but they were certain that no one could ever "capture" them in their pure state.

Robert Boyle argued eloquently that the "atomic philosophy," or as he sometimes called it, the "Corpuscular or Mechanic Philosophy," was a much better way of explaining how the world was put together. Boyle, whose every act was in harmony with his Christian beliefs, found the "Corpuscular Philosophy" to be completely acceptable. He believed that God had created the universe from "pure matter," which He had divided into corpuscles (tiny bodies) in continuous motion. The corpuscles, of which there were several different kinds, had definite shapes. They were all invisibly small, and solid. All matter which could be felt or seen was built up of clusters of these atoms which had joined together. These clusters could be rearranged by heat or by the action of acids or alkalies. The clusters could form even larger groups, or be broken apart into smaller clusters as their motion brought them together or separated them. Changes in the sizes of these groups changed their physical and chemical properties as well.

The sensible explanations which could be given

with the atomic philosophy can be well illustrated. The 17th-century chemists had difficulty in explaining why certain chemical salts became wet as they stood exposed to the air. The alchemists spoke vaguely of "sympathy" or natural pull which the salt exerted on water. Boyle's explanation was that clusters of water atoms in the air were brought to the salt in the course of their constant motion. These clusters passed through openings of the proper size in the clusters of salt atoms. The salts became wet for this reason, and not out of "sympathy." This is a logical, natural explanation based on simple and nonmysterious properties of matter. Boyle argued for his beliefs in the same scientific language which the natural philosophers used.

Boyle, of course, had no proof that these atoms or clusters of atoms were real. They offered a convenient and uncomplicated mechanical explanation like that used in the mechanical philosophy spreading throughout Europe. It could easily account for many different happenings, such as the heating-up of an iron nail when it was struck hard with a hammer. Boyle's explanation was that the hammer's motion was transferred to the nail, and as a result, the corpuscles of the nail moved more rapidly. The heat of the nail merely reflected the speed of the particles of the nail which, hitting against one's fingers, gave the sensation of heat.

Compare this answer with the statement that heat

was some sort of "element" which had an independent existence. Try to explain the heating of a cold nail when struck with a cold hammer by referring to an imaginary kind of heat. (It is much easier to explain this phenomenon in terms of motion being transferred from atom to atom.)

Despite Robert Boyle's intense study of chemistry and his defense of an atomic theory, his idea of what the chemical elements were like was far from the theories of modern chemistry. The approximately one hundred *elements* known today are defined as *substances which cannot be changed into simpler substances by ordinary chemical or physical means.* Everyone knows of such elements as iron, gold, silver, copper, oxygen, lead, tin, and helium. Few have heard of promethium, gadolinium, cesium, and cerium. These too are elements. Boyle's definition of an element is deceivingly modern in tone:

> I now mean by Elements, as those Chymists that speak plainest do by their Principles, certain Primitive and Simple, or perfectly unmingled bodies; which not being made of any other bodies, or of one another, are the ingredients of which all those call'd perfectly mixed bodies [compounds] are immediately compounded, and into which they are ultimately resolved.

When first read, this sounds like the modern definition of an element, but Boyle was really writing about something quite different. He believed, as we have already seen, that the atoms of his elements were solid bodies, and that these elements could be converted into other elements with the right kind of chemical treatment.

This, of course, has little in common with modern ideas. Each element is known to be made up of a single kind of atom which, in turn, is formed by a unique combination of certain smaller particles called electrons, protons, and neutrons. The atom of oxygen, for example, with its eight electrons, eight protons, and eight neutrons, differs from the atom of nitrogen, which is made of seven electrons, seven protons, and seven neutrons. It differs even more from the atom of aluminum, which contains thirteen electrons, thirteen protons, and fourteen neutrons.

When atoms of two different elements combine, the compound which is formed has properties which are quite unlike the properties of the uncombined elements. For example, hydrogen and oxygen are gases at room temperature and at normal atmospheric pressure, yet hydrogen combines explosively with oxygen to form liquid water. Under the proper chemical conditions, a compound may be broken apart to restore elements to their original form. When an electric current is passed through liquid water, the water changes back into the hydrogen and oxygen gases from which it was formed.

During the 17th and nearly all of the 18th century, no one, including Boyle, thought in these terms, and the first chemically useful description of atoms and elements was proposed in 1801 by John Dalton (1766–1844), a famous English chemist. Hundreds of chemists had spent more than a century of hard and often fruitless work trying to solve the mysteries of chemical substances before Dalton opened a whole new world of theory and experimentation with *his* atomic theory.

Despite Boyle's inability to explain how elements combine, he *was* able to show that the explanations of chemical action proposed by the alchemists and the Paracelsans were completely worthless. Isaac Newton was quick to accept Boyle's "atoms" as the building blocks of matter, and as a result, the men of the 18th century spoke of atoms instead of the alchemist's "elements."

Robert Boyle's acceptance of alchemy, or the transmutation of metals, was sensible, at least according to his beliefs about the structure of the chemical elements. He believed that gold and silver were made of the same kind of matter, and differed only in the ways in which their corpuscles were attached to each other. Therefore, he was convinced that he should be able to rearrange these corpuscles with the proper amount of heat and the right kind of chemicals, and in this way he would succeed in changing silver into gold or vice versa.

His praise of the virtues of the groundsel packet worn about the body to cure disease was also quite reasonable. After all, he *had* demonstrated that many solid substances gave off "steams," especially when they were heated. Could not the "steams" from groundsel exert a chemically healing effect when the groundsel was heated by touching the skin? The corpuscles of groundsel would penetrate the openings between the clusters of skin atoms, and once in the body, would do their work. Boyle, however, never tried to test this idea experimentally. Considering the crude facilities and equipment available to him, experiments for this purpose would have been worthless.

Robert Boyle, a 17th-century man with a strong infusion of the future, spoke and thought in a chemical language which is understandable today. Yet, despite his considerable knowledge of chemistry, he believed that when a plant was watered, some of the water was changed into soil. He even performed an experiment which "proved" this claim. He also thought that the water which was absorbed into the plant was immediately transmuted into the living tissue of the plant. We know today that water supplies the plant with elements which are necessary for growth, but a long and complicated series of chemical reactions must first occur before the plant builds these elements into its own living tissue.

Boyle would probably not have accepted the argument that plant growth is much more complicated a process than it seemed to be. According to his theoretical framework, the formation of plant tissue directly out of water was a reasonable expectation, certainly as reasonable as the transmutation of metals. Boyle always tried to act logically and sanely, relying on mechanical explanations, and, in most cases, on experimentation for his facts. But, experimentation sometimes led him into mistaken hypotheses and errors of interpretation.

The major obstacle to changing chemistry into a real science was that too little was known about how chemical compounds formed and how they changed. Even Boyle's genius could not invent an effective theory to explain and predict chemical reaction. This was too much to expect of any 17th-century scientist.

Chapter Five

The Man and His Times

Robert Boyle is one of the brightest names in the history of the sciences. With the exception of Isaac Newton, he was the foremost English scientist up to the end of the 18th century. Why should *he*, a man of high rank and wealth, have become so deeply interested in science when many of his noble friends and relatives spent their lives pursuing luxury? Why was he so dedicated to chemistry, a science scorned by the philosophers of his time? How could he ever have had the time and found the space to do the thousands of experiments he described in nearly a hundred articles and books? What was there in his life which made him what he was?

These questions are, of course, impossible to answer with certainty; but we do have some clues.

73

Boyle was a member of a very wealthy family, and, as he once remarked, to follow a career in science "requires a purse as well as a brain." Wealth *was* important. But the fact that he was the last of his father's sons is also significant. If Robert had been one of the older sons, he would have been forced to maintain the family estates and to take part in political and military activities. As the seventh son, there were no pressures to do that which he wished to avoid.

It is also significant that Boyle never accepted a title of nobility. If he had been a man of title, he could never have associated with the tradesmen and common workers from whom he gained an immense store of practical knowledge. His social position and wealth, however, gave him great influence in England, and all avenues to make his work easier were open to him.

His father, Richard Boyle, had risen by his own personality, ability, and ruthlessness from near-poverty to the high rank of first Earl of Cork. He was probably the wealthiest man in Ireland. He owned many thousands of acres of farmland, an iron-works, mines, and quarries, and even manufactured weapons. He carried on extensive trade with many European countries, and came to know influential men throughout all Europe.

Katherine Fenton Boyle, Robert's mother, was a devoted and charming lady who died when Robert was very young. Robert was the fourteenth child, the seventh son, and the next to the youngest of the Boyle children. He was born on January 25th, 1627, on the family estate of Lismore in Munster, Ireland. His father, who was then 61, loved Robert deeply, and Robert was destined to become his favorite son. He looked like the Earl of Cork. He was tall and wiry, full of energy, and strong-willed. He even seemed to think and act like his father, although their careers were so completely different.

Throughout his life, Robert was pale and thin, so strongly affected by even slight changes of temperature that he often changed his clothing hourly to match the temperature. Despite the repeated illnesses he suffered, he drove himself to long and exhausting work by the sheer power of his strong will. His eyes were weak and always troublesome, yet he read continually. He dressed plainly, despite the fact that his wealthy friends clothed themselves in silks and elaborate garments, and he ate only enough to sustain life.

His childhood was unfortunate, not only because his mother died when he was young, but because he stuttered and never completely overcame this handicap. This is probably one of the reasons that he shunned public affairs, and always spoke softly and unemotionally, in carefully measured tones.

When Robert was 9, he and his brother Francis were sent to Eton, one of England's famous "public" schools. (In England, public school is the name for a private school.) The Earl of Cork thought highly of Sir Henry Wotton, the head of Eton, and decided that his boys should be educated there. After a hazardous voyage from Ireland across pirate-infested waters, the boys were enrolled under the direct care of headmaster John Harrison, in whose house they lived. Harrison excited in Robert so strong a desire to learn that the boy had to be torn away from his beloved books to go outside to play. Despite his devotion to study, Robert was always on the friendliest of terms with his fellow students.

John Harrison, who opened Robert's eyes to the joy of learning, soon retired. The strict disciplinarian who took his place believed that the memorization and recitation of Latin texts was the key to learning, and Boyle's enjoyable days at Eton turned into a nightmare. After three years, the Earl of Cork was finally persuaded to take the boys out of Eton. Soon after, two of the older brothers returned from three years of European travel under the guidance of a Swiss tutor named Marcombes.

During the summer of 1639, Robert was tutored by Mr. Marcombes. When the English king, Charles I, invaded Scotland that year, the Earl of Cork volunteered the assistance of his sons, including Robert, who was only 12 at that time. Francis, however, fell ill just before the invasion and was forced to remain at home. Robert also stayed at home in order to take care of Francis and to look after the estate while the others fought the Scots.

After Francis recovered, he and Robert sailed for the "Grand Tour," a leisurely visit to the important cities of Europe which was to complete their education. For five years, from 1639 to 1644, they were in the good hands of Mr. Marcombes, at first in Switzerland and later in France and Italy.

In Switzerland, the boys lived in Marcombes' house in Geneva, one of the largest cities of the country. Robert happily studied logic, speech, algebra, geometry, French, and Latin. Because he was a "gentleman," he was taught to dance, to fence, and to play tennis. He cared little for dancing, but loved the fencing and the tennis.

Soon after he passed his thirteenth birthday in Geneva, an event occurred which profoundly changed his life. During a summer storm, he was so frightened by the violent flashes of lightning and the strong winds and thunder claps that he thought the Day of Judgment had come. He imagined that he was pitifully unprepared to meet his Maker, and resolved that he would henceforth lead a religious and blameless life should he survive the horror of that night. From that moment, he lived a truly faultless life. He shunned the dissipation, the gambling, and the wild life of the wealthy, holding fast to his vows to lead a Christian life.

Boyle gave a large share of his time to the study of religion, but he did not accept religion uncritically, for he accepted nothing on faith alone. He always tried to find logical and worthy reasons for accepting and acting on the precepts of Protestantism. When offered high positions in the Anglican Church, he refused to be ordained because he believed he was unworthy of such offices. He felt deeply that he would do far more for his church as a layman than as a priest. The sciences to which he contributed so fully were to him evidences of God's goodness and handiwork. His discoveries and theories were his personal contributions to the advancement of God's work.

After leaving Switzerland, he and Francis visited Italy. They lived in Florence for months, studying Italian, visiting factories and tradesmen, seeing the sights, and reading the works of the new scientists, including Galileo, who died in Florence in 1642 while Robert was living there. Robert was enchanted by the new philosophy of which Galileo was one of the pioneers, and it is probable that he first dedicated himself to science at this time when he was 15 years old.

From Italy, the two boys traveled to France. Because their father, the Earl of Cork, was unable to

send money, they were forced to return to Geneva with Mr. Marcombes. After two years, there was still no money. In desperation, and fearing the worst, they sold some small jewels and managed to find their way back to England in the summer of 1644, to discover that the nation was in a hopeless state of confusion. The Royalists who supported King Charles I were at war with the supporters of the English Parliament, who sought to reduce the King's power.

On his return to London at the age of 17, Robert learned that his father had died the year before. His family was unaware of his arrival, and he did not know at first where they were living. By accident, he met his sister Katherine in that great city. Katherine, who was married to an English lord, was wealthy and could give him shelter. Through her friendship with the leading men of those troubled times, Robert was able to secure control of *some* estates in Ireland which his father had left him. The income from these lands was sufficient to support his every need.

In 1646, Robert, at some danger to his life because armed bands of men patrolled the roads, managed to make his way to a family estate at Stalbridge which had been half destroyed in the war. He remained there for six years in order to restore its former prosperity. Despite his lonely existence, or perhaps because of it, he escaped involvement in risky political action and found time enough to pursue his studies. He was particularly attracted to both natural philosophy and to agriculture. The latter, of course, was of great importance at Stalbridge. The improvement of agriculture had been strongly urged by the famous writer, Francis Bacon, who always looked with approval on knowledge which was of practical value. At Stalbridge, Robert planned and carried out his first experiments in chemistry.

During his few months in London, he had met Samuel Hartlib, a refugee from religious persecution in Germany. Hartlib, who was deeply interested in science, was full of schemes for improving and enriching man's life. Hartlib knew all the important scientists and artisans of his time. He carried on an immense correspondence with these men, both in England and on the continent. Robert Boyle, an idealist, was attracted by Hartlib's unselfish devotion to the goal of improving man's life by applying scientific knowledge. Before long, Robert had become a member of an "Invisible college," a group of men who sought to apply this new philosophy. At Stalbridge, he continued to correspond with the members of this "College," and occasionally he visited them in London.

Although life at Stalbridge was quiet and peaceful, much of England was still in the throes of the civil war, and it was not until King Charles I was executed by the Parliamentarians in 1649 that relative tranquility returned to England. In 1652 Robert was forced to leave Stalbridge to seek the return of *all* of the estates in Ireland which had been left to him by his father. Years of turmoil in England and Ireland had mixed up the ownership of many homes, and Robert struggled for two years to make good his claims.

Without books and apparatus to continue his experiments, Robert was troubled and unhappy. He managed, however, to visit mines and metal refineries, to study anatomy and to perform dissections of animals, to mingle with metalworkers, glassblowers, and other artisans, and to observe most carefully the plants and animals around him. In 1654 Robert moved to Oxford to be closer to the scientists and the other learned men with whom he loved to talk and work. He no longer needed the quiet of Stalbridge. At the great university of Oxford, there lived such men as John Wallis, the mathematician; Seth Ward, the astronomer; Christopher Wren, the architect; and Robert Hooke, who, though still an undergraduate, had already established a scientific reputation.

The move to Oxford was a turning point in Boyle's life. He associated daily with men of great scientific ability. He tried out his ideas on them and listened to their criticisms. He argued with them, and thereby improved his own scientific skills and knowledge. Scientists rarely develop their talents to the fullest unless they are close to men whose interests they

share. The great scientists have, more often than not, been in the very center of intellectual ferment, both stimulating it and being stimulated by it.

At Oxford, Boyle burst the bonds of the "amateur" scientist. Although he did not have to earn a livelihood from his work, and he had never studied the sciences at the university, he was an accomplished scientist. His self-discipline, which was coupled with a never-ending stream of ideas, a more or less methodical way of planning research and of directing his laboratory assistants, marked him as a true professional.

It was at Oxford that the famous experiments with the vacuum pump were first performed. He probably learned more with the vacuum pump than did any other scientist using this tool.

Strangely enough, his first important book was about religion rather than science. Entitled *Seraphic Love*, it appeared almost by accident in 1659. Boyle, following a general practice in Europe, wrote long letters which were circulated among his friends. These letters described his current investigations. Occasionally, they fell into unscrupulous hands and were printed without his permission. In 1659, a printer came to him with a copy of *Seraphic Love*, which was the title of one of these letters. The printer knew that there were some errors in the copy which he had obtained, and he asked Boyle for permission to publish an accurate edition of the letter. Boyle

agreed to the printer's request, and the letter was soon published as a book. With this start, book soon followed book at the rate of one or more a year.

When the monarchy was restored to England in 1660, Robert Boyle quickly became a favorite of King Charles II. He was often invited to the royal court. Not only was he a son of one of England's greatest families, he was also acknowledged as England's greatest scientist. When he was rewarded by the King with new lands in Ireland, he gave the money to spread the Protestant doctrine to Ireland and America. He was appointed by the King to head a society for "Propagating the Gospel in New England," a post which he took very seriously. In his will, he left a large grant to both Harvard College and to William and Mary College to spread *The Faith* among the Indians of the new world. He became a member of the Board of Directors of the famous East India Company, which had immense business interests in India. Robert Boyle accepted this time-consuming duty for two reasons. He saw in it an opportunity to support missionary activities in India, and, at the same time, to gather information about the plants and animals of that strange exotic land.

In 1664 Robert Boyle became a director of the Board of the Royal Mines, which had been organized to encourage exploration for valuable minerals. This was an ideal task for him. He saw in it still another way to harness chemistry and natural philosophy to help his fellow man. He toured England seeking new sources of economically important minerals, and on his death he left his excellent collection of minerals to the Royal Society of London.

The favor in which he was held at the Court of King Charles II was to be of enormous help to English science. As the nation settled back to enjoy the benefits of peace, the scientists who had fled London during the upheavals began to return. In order to promote "experimental philosophy," they began to meet informally in 1660, and soon decided that they would be more effective if they founded a society for that purpose. To gain added prestige and, if possible, money for their organization, they sought assistance from the King. In 1662, the King granted the group a charter as "The Royal Society of London for Promoting Natural Knowledge." This Society, one of the leaders in the world of science, has amply fulfilled the hopes and dreams of its founders.

Robert Boyle rarely served the Royal Society as an officer, preferring instead to report regularly on his research, to give ingenious demonstrations, and to discuss the latest developments in science with his colleagues. At his recommendation, his former assistant, Robert Hooke, became the Demonstrator of the Society. In this role, Hooke was responsible for preparing interesting and thought-provoking experiments at each of the weekly meetings.

Boyle supported in every way he could the purpose of the Society, which was, "Further promoting by the authority of experiments the sciences of natural things and of useful arts, to the glory of God the Creator, and the advantage of the human race." Occasionally, he served as President of the Society, but not for more than a month at a time. Despite the fact that he lived in Oxford until 1668, Boyle attended nearly all of the weekly meetings. When he was prevented by illness or business from attending, he sent questions for discussion to the Society and tried to keep the members informed of his own work.

In 1680, when he was again elected President of the Society, he refused because he could not, in all conscience, accept certain new oaths to which he would have had to swear. Despite this refusal, his devotion to the Society remained firm, and he continued to attend regularly.

When he moved to London in 1668, he continued his researches in a well-equipped laboratory in his new home. To his dismay, he discovered that he had become an international celebrity. Visitors came from all over Europe to see and meet the great chemist, whether or not they knew anything about science. Boyle was soon so exasperated with these constant interruptions to his work that he published a notice that visitors would not be received on Tuesday, Wednesday, Friday, and Saturday afternoons. He also posted a conspicuous sign outside his door stating his visiting hours. The guests, both invited and uninvited, came not just to talk, but to see him demonstrate his famous pump, and to gaze in awe at his startling chemistry experiments.

He received these men graciously, but he particularly welcomed the many young men who came to his laboratory to beg for the opportunity to serve as his assistants. Denis Papin, who had assisted the renowned Christiaan Huygens in Paris, spent many months with Boyle. He helped Boyle with some experiments, but he also worked to perfect a device he called a "digester," which was an early kind of pressure cooker. Papin demonstrated his "digester" to the Royal Society in 1682. He cooked a "philosophical supper" of "beef-bone jelly, fish reduced to a jelly, and pigeons" for the members. Guillaume Homberg, a French chemist, took Boyle's ideas back to France, and was instrumental in changing the whole approach of French chemistry. These were but two of Boyle's assistants. Robert Boyle always advised and encouraged these young scientists and thus helped to mold the style and content of chemistry in England and Europe for more than a century.

His incredible capacity for hard work is all the more admirable because he was often seriously ill. His eyesight continually troubled him. He suffered from malaria, kidney stones, and frequent colds. None of these conditions could do more than slow him down. In 1670, however, he was paralyzed by a

stroke so severe that for many months he was unable to raise either hand. Even though he could neither read nor write, he dictated in his soft, strained voice to his secretary, and somehow kept several assistants continually at work in the laboratory. For nearly a full year he was confined to bed. By will power alone, he struggled to move his arms and legs and eventually, he was able to move around almost as well as before his illness. The long history of disease, however, so weakened him that in 1691, when he was 64, he knew the end was near at hand. On July 18 of that year he made a final will giving his property to relatives, friends, dependents, charitable organizations, and, of course, to his beloved Royal Society.

Robert Boyle died on December 30, 1691, a week after the death of his favorite sister Katherine. He was buried in the Church of St. Martin's-in-the-fields, next to Katherine. Years later, this church was demolished. No trace of his burial place exists to mark the last resting place of a great humanitarian and scientist, but his eminence in 17th-century England is well illustrated by the words of John Evelyn, a well-known diarist of that time, who knew him well:

> This last week died that pious admirable Christian, excellent philosopher, and my worthy friend, Mr. Boyle, aged about 65—a great loss to all that knew him, and to the public.

His courtesy to his peers and to those who worked for him was well known. His reputation for truthfulness and sincerity in all his affairs is summarized in the words of another mourner:

> The sweetest modesty, the noblest discoveries and the sincerest relations, the greatest self-denial and the greatest love of men, the profoundest insight into philosophy and nature, the most devout, affectionate sense of God and religion [are shown by him].

He was sometimes criticized for his scientific beliefs. He was never condemned as a human being. As one of his contemporaries said:

> He was a mighty promoter of all pious and good works. He was a mighty chemist.

Glossary

Accademia del Cimento. The Experimental Academy, an early scientific society whose members included Galileo, Torricelli, and Viviani. The Accademia was founded in 1657 and continued for ten years.

Accademia dei Lincei. The Academy of the Lynxes, one of the first scientific societies, was founded in 1603 in Rome. The lynx, which is a kind of wildcat, was a symbol of the clear vision which came from studying science.

Acetic acid. The acid found in vinegar. Its chemical formula is CH_3COOH.

Acid. A chemical substance which turns litmus red, usually has a sour taste, and reacts with certain metals to give off hydrogen gas.

Aether. An invisible and undetectable substance which was said to fill all space, even a "vacuum." The hypothesis of the "aether" is now considered to be unnecessary.

Air pressure. The weight of a column of air. The pressure of air at sea level is 14.7 pounds for each square inch of surface on which the air column rests. This pressure will support a column of mercury about 30 inches high.

Alchemy. The "science" which attempted to transmute metals into gold, to lengthen human life, and to find the "Philosopher's Stone."

Alcohol. Also known as ethyl alcohol, a common chemical substance whose chemical formula is C_2H_5OH.

Alkali. A chemical substance which turns litmus blue and reacts with acids in solution to form a salt. For example: ammonia, an alkali, reacts with hydrochloric acid to form ammonium chloride, NH_4Cl, a salt.

Aluminum oxide. A chemical compound of aluminum and oxygen whose formula is Al_2O_3.

Ammonia. An alkali whose formula is NH_3.

Aqua fortis. An old name for concentrated nitric acid.

Aqua regia. A mixture of concentrated hydrochloric and nitric acids which is strong enough to dissolve gold.

Atmosphere. The total cover of air surrounding the earth.

Atomic philosophy. The belief that matter was composed of atoms, and that the behavior of the different kinds of matter could be explained by the ways in which atoms combined.

Barometer. An instrument for measuring changing air pressure.

Boyle's Law. A statement describing the change in volume of a gas when the pressure on the gas changes. The law states that if the pressure on a gas increases, the volume of the gas decreases correspondingly. If the pressure on the gas decreases, the volume of the gas increases accordingly.

Chemical reaction. The change which occurs when chemical substances affect one another. There is usually a change in the appearance of the substances, and there are changes in the ways in which they behave and in the energy they contain as a result of the reaction.

Chemistry. The science that deals with the elements of which all substances are composed, the different ways in which these elements can be combined, and the ways in which these elements and their combinations behave.

Chloride. A chemical compound which contains one or more chlorine atoms, as in mercuric chloride, $HgCl_2$.

Compound. A substance made up of two or more elements in a definite proportion by weight. A compound can be broken down into its elements by ordinary chemical means.

Corpuscular philosophy. See *Atomic philosophy.*

Element. Today defined as a form of matter which cannot be broken down into simpler forms by ordinary chemical means. More than a hundred elements are known today. Iron, hydrogen, chloride, and oxygen are examples.

Early definitions of chemical elements were quite different.

Eponym. A person's name given to a scientific law, process or piece of apparatus.

Funiculus. A thin, invisible cord which was said by some 17th-century critics of Robert Boyle to be attached to the mercury column of a torricellian barometer, and to be strong enough to support a column of mercury 30 inches high. The funiculus is now a forgotten hypothesis.

Hooke's Law. In one version, it is the statement that if a spiral spring is pulled down a certain distance by a weight, the spring will be pulled down twice as far by twice the weight.

Hydrochloric acid. A strong acid whose chemical formula is HCl.

Hypothesis. A suggested explanation of observed facts.

Iatrochemistry. The "science" through which certain chemists sought to prepare medicines which would cure all diseases. Its founder was Paracelsus.

Indicator. A chemical substance which changes color in the presence of acids or alkalis. Litmus paper and phenolphthalein are well-known indicators.

Law. A description, usually given in mathematical terms, of certain regularly occurring scientific phenomena. Boyle's Law, which describes the changes in volume of a gas when the pressure on the gas changes, and Hooke's Law, which describes the changes in the length of a spiral spring when different weights are attached to the spring, are examples of scientific laws.

Litmus paper. A chemical indicator which turns blue in the presence of an alkali, and pink in the presence of an acid.

Mechanic philosophy. See *Atomic philosophy.*

Mercury. A silver liquid metal of high density.

Mercury sublimate. Mercuric chloride, a dangerous poison whose chemical formula is $HgCl_2$.

Natural philosopher. An early name for a scientist.

Nitrate. A group of atoms containing one nitrogen and three oxygen atoms which act as a unit in certain chemical compounds.

Nitric acid. A strong acid whose chemical formula is HNO_3.

Normal air pressure. The pressure of the air at sea level which will just balance a column of mercury approximately 30 inches (29.92 inches exactly) high. This is equal to 14.7 pounds for each square inch of surface.

Oil of vitriol. A common name for concentrated sulphuric acid.

Phenomenon. An unusual happening or experience.

Philosopher's Stone. A magical substance believed by alchemists to have been able to transmute (change) base metals (lead, copper, iron) into gold or silver.

Phosphoric acid. A chemical compound whose formula is H_3PO_4.

Phosphoric oxide. A chemical compound of phosphorus and oxygen.

Physics. The science of the behavior of matter and energy which include electricity, heat, force, atomic structure, and motion.

Piston. A kind of rod used in the vacuum pump to pull air out of a container.

Pneumatics. A branch of physics which studies the properties of liquids and gases.

Potash. Potassium carbonate, a chemical compound with the formula K_2CO_3. Potassium carbonate is an alkali.

Potassium arsenate. A chemical salt whose formula is K_3AsO_4.

Pressure. The force acting on a definite area. The normal pressure of air is 14.7 pounds for each square inch of surface exposed to the air.

Pump. A machine for lifting liquids in a pipe. (See *Vacuum pump*)

Receiver. The container of a vacuum pump from which the air is removed.

Royal Society. The Royal Society of London, chartered by King Charles II in 1662 to promote scientific study. This Society, which is still in existence, is one of the most important scientific societies in the world.

Salt. A product of the reaction between an acid and an alkali. Sodium chloride and potassium nitrate are examples of salts.

Silver chloride. A chemical salt whose formula is AgC1.

Sodium carbonate. A chemical salt whose formula is Na_2CO_3. Sodium carbonate is alkaline when it is dissolved in water.

Sulphate. A group of atoms containing one sulphur and four oxygen atoms which acts as a unit in certain chemical compounds.

Sulphuric acid. A strong acid whose chemical formula is H_2SO_4.

Syrup of violets. An indicator discovered by Robert Boyle.

Touchstone. A black stone which gives a golden streak when rubbed by gold. Often used by alchemists to test the products of their laboratories.

Transmutation. The process of changing base metals such as lead and iron into precious metals such as gold and silver.

Vacuum. A space which contains few or no molecules or atoms.

Vacuum pump. A machine which removes air from a receiver (container) in order to form a vacuum.

Index